TO THE LEADER

In *The Wesley Challenge: 21 Days to a More Authentic Faith*, Chris Folmsbee explores twenty-one questions John Wesley used in Oxford, England, with the group that was nicknamed "The Holy Club." By exploring each of these questions, both individually and as a group, participants may find a more sustainable union with God through everyday practices. Growing in the lives God intended for us involves both talking about and living out the teachings of Jesus. Each of the three sessions in this study addresses seven of the questions, grouped into three categories: Relationship with God, Relationship with Self, and Relationship with Others. Since Wesley originally intended the practices resulting from engaging these questions to be lived out in a group of Christian brothers and sisters, the challenges in this book are best explored in the context of a group.

In this study, Folmsbee challenges readers to the difficult questions of faith in practice. From "Do I go to bed on time?" to "Is Jesus real to me?" the questions touch every aspect of life and faith. As group leader, you will guide others in a process of discernment that will help you to come together around discussions of prayer, faithful living, relationships, and spirituality. This process is dependent on the guidance of the Holy Spirit. Scripture tells us that where two or three are gathered together, we can be assured of the presence of Christ, working in and through all those gathered.

As you prepare to lead, pray for that presence and expect that you will experience it.

This three-session study makes use of the following components:

- the book The Wesley Challenge: 21 Days to a More Authentic Faith by Chris Folmsbee
- this Leader Guide
- the video segments on the companion DVD

In addition to the study book, group members will also need Bibles and either a notebook or electronic tablet for journaling. Be sure to notify those interested in the study in advance so they may obtain copies of the book and read the introduction and Section 1 before the first session.

USING THIS GUIDE WITH YOUR GROUP

Because no two groups are alike, this guide is structured to give you flexibility and choice in tailoring the sessions for your group. The basic session format is designed for a fifty-minute Sunday school or other small-group session, with additional options for groups wanting to explore the text in more depth. Suggested time allotments are provided only as a general guide. Select ahead of time which activities and discussion questions your group will do, for how long, and in what order—adapting the material as you wish to meet the schedule and needs of your particular group. Depending on which activities you select, special preparation may be necessary. Instructions regarding preparation are provided at the beginning of each session plan.

BASIC SESSION FORMAT

Planning the Session (In Advance)

Session Goals

Section Summary

Biblical Foundation
Special Preparation

Facilitating the Session (50 minutes)

Welcome and Opening Prayer (3 minutes)
Video (10 minutes)
Biblical Foundation (5 minutes)
Week in Review (10 minutes)
Group Activity (20 minutes)
Ideas for Further Reflection (additional 30 minutes if needed)
Closing Prayer (2 minutes)

Two primary objectives undergird each group session: (1) In the Week in Review, participants will find help for understanding the material, moving through the individual exercises, and connecting their beliefs with practice; (2) in the Group Activity, group members will engage in conversation and activity that will deepen their understanding of the questions and their connection to the week's theme.

HELPFUL HINTS

Before you get started, here are a few helpful hints to equip you for preparing, shaping, and managing the group experience:

Preparing for the Session

- Pray for the leading of the Holy Spirit as you prepare for the study. Pray for discernment for yourself and for each member of the study group.

- Before each session, read the book section and familiarize yourself with the content.

- Choose the session elements you will use during the group session, including the specific discussion questions you plan to cover. Be prepared, however, to

9

adjust the session as group members interact and as questions arise. Prepare carefully, but allow space for the Holy Spirit to move in and through the group members and through you as facilitator.

- If you plan to use video clips or music suggestions, obtain appropriate projection equipment and test it before the session in which you plan to use it.

- Prepare the space where the group will meet so that the environment will enhance the learning process. Ideally, group members should be seated around a table or in a circle so that all can see one another. Movable chairs are best because the group will often form pairs or small groups for discussion.

- Bring a supply of Bibles for those who forget to bring their own. Provide a variety of translations.

- For most sessions you will also need an easel with paper and markers, a whiteboard, and markers, or some other means of posting group questions and responses.

Shaping the Learning Environment

- Begin and end on time.

- Establish a welcoming space. Consider the room temperature, access to amenities, hospitality, outside noise, and privacy. Consider using a small cross or candle as a focal point for times of prayer.

- Create a climate of openness, encouraging group members to participate as they feel comfortable. Some participants may be uncomfortable or embarrassed about sharing their experiences. Be on the lookout for signs of discomfort in those who may be silent, and encourage them to express their thoughts and feelings honestly. Assure the group members that passing on a question is always acceptable.

- Remember that some people will jump right in with answers and comments, while others need time to process what is being discussed.

- If you notice that some group members seem never to be able to enter the conversation, ask them if they have thoughts to share. Give everyone a chance to talk, but keep the conversation moving. Moderate to prevent a few individuals from doing all the talking.

- Make use of the exercises that invite sharing in pairs. Those who are reluctant to speak out in a group setting may be more comfortable sharing one-on-one and reporting back to the group. This can often be an effective means of helping people grow more comfortable sharing in the larger setting. It also helps to avoid the dominance of the group by one or two participants (including you!).

- If no one answers at first during discussions, do not be afraid of silence. Help the group become comfortable with waiting. If no one responds, try reframing the language of the question. If no responses are forthcoming, venture an answer yourself and ask for comments.

- Model openness as you share with the group. Group members will follow your example. If you limit your sharing to a surface level, others will follow suit.

- Encourage multiple answers or responses before moving on.

- Ask, "Why?" or "Why do you believe that?" or "Can you say more about that?" to help continue a discussion and give it greater depth.

- Affirm others' responses with comments such as "great" or "thanks" or "good insight"—especially if it's the first time someone has spoken during the group session.

- Monitor your own contributions. If you are doing most of the talking, back off so that you do not train the group to listen rather than speak up.

- Remember that you do not have all the answers. Your job is to keep the discussion going and encourage participation.

Managing the Session

- Honor the time schedule. If a session is running longer than expected, get consensus from the group before continuing beyond the agreed-upon ending time.
- When someone arrives late or *must* leave early, pause the session *briefly* to welcome them or bid them farewell. Changes in the makeup of the group change the dynamics of the discussion and need to be acknowledged. Every group member is important to the entire group.
- Involve group members in various aspects of the group session, such as saying prayers or reading the Scripture passage.
- As always in discussions that may involve personal sharing, confidentiality is essential. Group members should never pass along stories that have been shared in the group. Remind the group members at each session: confidentiality is crucial to the success of this study.

Session 1

RELATIONSHIP WITH GOD: AN UPWARD FOCUS

Session 1

RELATIONSHIP WITH GOD: AN UPWARD FOCUS

PLANNING THE SESSION

Session Goals

As a result of conversations and activities connected with this session, group members should begin to:

- Consider the first seven questions about the relationship with God.
- Understand through an exploration of these questions how they can enrich and enliven their relationship with God.
- Examine the relationship between prayer and daily life.

Section Summary

Section 1 explores the first seven of John Wesley's twenty-one questions. These questions address the theme of "Relationship with God: an Upward Focus." In these questions, Wesley sets forth a challenge to become who God intended us to be. Through this material, we reflect on prayer, Scripture, and our relationship with Jesus. The person and work of Jesus provide the model for the life God meant for us to live.

Biblical Foundation

"I am the true vine, and my Father is the vineyard keeper. He removes any of my branches that don't produce fruit, and he trims any branch that produces fruit so that it will produce even more fruit. You are already trimmed because of the word I have spoken to you. Remain in me, and I will remain in you. A branch can't produce fruit by itself, but must remain in the vine. Likewise, you can't produce fruit unless you remain in me. I am the vine; you are the branches. If you remain in me and I in you, then you will produce much fruit. Without me, you can't do anything. If you don't remain in me, you will be like a branch that is thrown out and dries up. Those branches are gathered up, thrown into a fire, and burned. If you remain in me and my words remain in you, ask for whatever you want and it will be done for you. My Father is glorified when you produce much fruit and in this way prove that you are my disciples."

John 15:1-8

Jesus told them, "When you pray, say:

'Father, uphold the holiness of your name.
Bring in your kingdom.
Give us the bread we need for today.
Forgive us our sins,
    for we also forgive everyone who has wronged us.
And don't lead us into temptation.'"

Luke 11:2-4

From now on, brothers and sisters, if anything is excellent and if anything is admirable, focus your thoughts on these things: all that is true, all that is holy, all that is just, all that is pure, all that is lovely, and all that is worthy of praise.

Philippians 4:8

Special Preparation

- Provide writing paper and pens for those who may need them. Also have Bibles available for those who do not bring one.
- Make sure all participants have a copy of the book *The Wesley Challenge: 21 Days to a More Authentic Faith*. Invite them to read the introduction and Section 1 in advance of the first session.
- Have available large sheets of blank paper to attach to the wall or a large whiteboard and markers for group activity.
- Bring index cards to distribute for group activity.
- As the leader, go over the session in advance and select or adapt the activities you think will work best for your group in the time allotted. Consider your own responses to questions you will pose to the group.
- Make nametags available if desired.

FACILITATING THE SESSION

Welcome and Opening Prayer (3 minutes)

As participants arrive, welcome them to the study and invite them to make use of one of the available Bibles if they did not bring one. Introduce yourself. You may want to share why you are excited about facilitating this study of *The Wesley Challenge: 21 Days to a More Authentic Faith*. If you sense that the participants in your group do not know each other well, allow time during this first session for them to introduce themselves and share something about their relationship with the church, for example the name of a Sunday school class to which they belong, a mission project they support, or which worship service they attend. Extend a special welcome to those who do not regularly attend your church.

Offer the prayer below, pray one of your own, or invite a group member to pray.

Everlasting God,
Who is your beloved Son,
Who is the King of the whole world;
Who wills to restore all things to be made new;
Who gives Mercy to all the people of all the nations,
Who with you, God, lives and reigns for ever
we ask that we find Jesus to be more real every day.

Video (10 minutes)

Play the video for session 1. In this segment, Chris Folmsbee introduces the Wesley Challenge, gives the history of John Wesley's twenty-one questions, and presents the first set of seven questions, focusing on "Do I pray about the money I spend?"

Choose from the following for a brief discussion:

- Wesley's motto was, "Earn all you can, save all you can, give all you can." Do you think this is a good premise to live by? Why or why not?
- Do you consider spending money to be a spiritual activity? Why or why not?
- What do you think of the author's contention, "The money I possess is not mine. It is God's money"?

Biblical Foundation (5 minutes)

Section 1 cites John 15:1-8 to describe the relationship between human beings and Jesus. Read the passage aloud and consider the following questions:

- Jesus says that there are two kinds of branches. What are they, and what do they symbolize?

- What does it mean to "remain" in Jesus? Do humans have a choice to remain, unlike branches?

- Jesus says, "My Father is glorified when you produce much fruit and in this way prove that you are my disciples." What does it mean to "produce much fruit"? In practical terms, what human "fruit" proves that they are disciples of Jesus?

Week in Review (10 minutes)

The seven questions in Section 1 explore the nature of our relationship with God through Jesus, prayer, and Scripture. Review the questions with the group:

1. Is Jesus real to me?
2. Am I enjoying prayer?
3. Do I insist upon doing something about which my conscience is uneasy?
4. Did the Bible live in me today?
5. Did I disobey God in anything?
6. Do I pray about the money I spend?
7. Do I give time for the Bible to speak to me every day?

Invite responses to a few of the prompts below:

- What was your experience moving through the questions this first week?

- Which ones stood out to you?

- Which were the most difficult to grapple with?

- Did any of them lead to a sense of transformation as you contemplated them?

- How did living the questions this week have an impact on your own relationship with God?

- What was your method of engaging the questions?
- Did you read the passages in the morning or the evening?

Group Activity (20 minutes)

The following section provides opportunities for discussion of the week's theme, Relationship with God, and the seven related questions. Choose from the following activities to find one that best fits your group dynamic.

Making Jesus Real

Have the following questions posted on a large sheet of paper (newsprint or poster paper) or whiteboard:

- When was the first time Jesus became more than just a name to you?
- When was the last time Jesus was more than just a name to you?

Invite participants into conversation in small groups of three or four. The questions are designed to help people think about how their relationship with God has evolved over time. This process helps us learn how to tell our faith stories and how to actively listen to and learn from the stories of others as all of our stories continue.

Give the small groups fifteen minutes to share their responses with one another. Remind them that as each person shares, the task of the listeners is to attend to and receive the story in prayerful silence. Remind them that each person should have the opportunity to share and that someone may choose not to share.

At the end of the fifteen minutes of small group time, invite the groups back together. Ask them to share insights gained from hearing one another's stories and from sharing their own. How has their faith changed and grown over time? What do the variety of faith stories tell us about the nature of God and our relationship with God and one another?

Make a Habit

List on a whiteboard or large sheet of paper any spiritual disciplines and practices you can identify. These could include prayer, reading and studying Scripture, worship, Holy Communion, acts of service and justice, and so on. How do these practices bring you closer to God? Which of these disciplines do you already practice? Which have become daily or weekly habits?

- What habits are part of your daily routine? How do these habits give your life structure?
- What habits related to your faith have you developed?
- How do your daily habits reveal your faith and values?
- How has asking these daily questions affected your spiritual life this week?
- What is most challenging about turning a spiritual practice into a spiritual habit?
- Read the following Scriptures: Acts 2:42-47; Galatians 5:22-23; 1 Thessalonians 5:17-24; James 5:13-18. What insight do they give about spiritual practices and habits?

The believers devoted themselves to the apostles' teaching, to the community, to their shared meals, and to their prayers. A sense of awe came over everyone. God performed many wonders and signs through the apostles. All the believers were united and shared everything. They would sell pieces of property and possessions and distribute the proceeds to everyone who needed them. Every day, they met together in the temple and ate in their homes. They shared food with gladness and simplicity. They praised God and demonstrated

21

God's goodness to everyone. The Lord added daily to the community those who were being saved.

Acts 2:42-47

But the fruit of the Spirit is love, joy, peace, patience, kindness, goodness, faithfulness, gentleness, and self-control. There is no law against things like this.

Galatians 5:22-23

Pray continually. Give thanks in every situation because this is God's will for you in Christ Jesus. Don't suppress the Spirit. Don't brush off Spirit-inspired messages, but examine everything carefully and hang on to what is good. Avoid every kind of evil. Now, may the God of peace himself cause you to be completely dedicated to him; and may your spirit, soul, and body be kept intact and blameless at our Lord Jesus Christ's coming. The one who is calling you is faithful and will do this.

1 Thessalonians 5:17-24

If any of you are suffering, they should pray. If any of you are happy, they should sing. If any of you are sick, they should call for the elders of the church, and the elders should pray over them, anointing them with oil in the name of the Lord. Prayer that comes from faith will heal the sick, for the Lord will restore them to health. And if they have sinned, they will be forgiven. For this reason, confess your sins to each other and pray for each other so that you may be healed. The prayer of the righteous person is powerful in what it can achieve. Elijah was a person just like us. When he earnestly prayed that it wouldn't rain, no rain fell for three and a half years. He prayed again, God sent rain, and the earth produced its fruit.

James 5:13-18

Listen Closely

Allow everyone time to reflect on an experience when he or she came to a greater understanding of someone after seeing things from that person's perspective. If people feel comfortable doing so, invite them to share this experience with the group.

Then have members of the group pair off. One person in each pair should spend exactly one minute describing to his or her partner one important faith experience. The partner should listen closely, and, afterward, repeat as closely as possible what he or she heard. Partners should repeat this process, this time with the roles reversed. Come back together as a group and discuss:

- How difficult was it for you to listen intently to your partner?
- How closely did you find you were able to retell your partner's faith story?
- Why is it important that we listen to and learn other people's stories?
- How might your interactions with people change if you took the time and effort to try to see from their perspective?
- In what ways did listening to and telling faith stories bring you closer to God?

The Living Bible

Distribute several index cards to each member of the group. Offer this instruction: On each card, list one way you see the Bible living in you today. Allow a few minutes for participants to do this individually, then invite volunteers to share from their lists and record responses on the board or a large sheet of paper. Pose the following questions for discussion:

- What does it mean to have the Bible "live in you"?
- Was it easy or difficult to find ways the Bible appears in your life?
- What Bible stories or passages feature most prominently in your spiritual life?

The Prayer of Jesus

Divide into pairs and read John 17. The author cites this prayer as giving insight and perspective into what Wesley meant when he asked, "Am I enjoying prayer?" Take ten minutes to read John 17 and think about whether Jesus enjoyed this prayer. What aspects of the prayer would have meant fulfillment for Jesus? What can we learn about prayer from this example? What might we mean by "enjoy" in this context that goes beyond the typical definition of joy or delight? To enjoy prayer is to have experiences of discovery within the practice. The author writes, "To 'enjoy' prayer is to experience God through realizing and remembering God, self, others, and the world, and at the same time trust the direction God desires for our lives."

Bible stories

How has your view of the Bible changed throughout your life? Do you value the Bible differently or relate to it differently from what you did when you were younger?

Divide into pairs and have each pair choose a Bible story learned as a child. As a team, write down the main elements of that story without looking at the text. Write down as much as you can remember. Try to recall what the main understanding of the story was when it was first encountered. Next, have each pair reread that story. What elements of the narrative do you find are missing? Did you add any details that weren't in the original version? What are your primary takeaways from this story at this point in your life? How has your life experience enriched your understanding of God's word?

Ideas for Further Reflection
(additional 30 minutes if needed)

Choose from the following questions to offer the class ways to reflect further on this week's seven questions in the week to come. Alternatively, these questions may be used to supplement the class discussion.

- After your group discussion, commit to making at least one change in your life to reorder it against temptations. Choose accountability partners within the group to help keep that change in place. Text or call each other throughout the week when a temptation is faced, or when encouragement is needed.

- Go around as a group and share a time when you felt a significant connection to God during prayer.

- If you are struggling to share your personal sins, use a 3-by-5 card or scrap of paper to write a prayer of confession to God. After each person has written on the card, shuffle the confessions, pass them out and have each person read the confession so that each person can hear his or her prayer to God.

- Were you raised in a household that prayed about spending money? Were you brought up in a way that reflects the Gain, Save, and Give principles or with a different perspective? What impact has your upbringing had on how you deal with money now? Share your observations with the group.

- Put together a Bible reading plan for your group this week. Choose a book of the Bible that you will all read before you meet again. Discuss what you will read each day. Encourage each other to look and listen for signs of Revelation, Illumination, and Imagination from God while reading, and have each member jot down impressions. When you gather again, share these impressions and the different ways that people heard God speak to them.

- If you are called to increase your participation in one of Wesley's principles related to money (and for most of us, that would be in either Save or Give), share your plans with the group. Hold each other accountable by asking one another about the commitments each week.

- Take turns sharing at least one area that you consistently struggle with. After each person has the chance to share, take time and pray for one another. Pray that God would grant you peace, strength, and faith.

- How would you currently answer the question, "Am I enjoying prayer?"

- Discuss the prayer practices you follow, as well as methods you might have tried and stopped.

- Discuss one area of your life that causes you an uneasy conscience. If you are struggling with a temptation that you are not comfortable sharing with the whole group, choose one or two members of the group to confide in.

- How did the Bible factor into your upbringing? Was it something that played center stage in your family's life, or did it sit on a shelf, collecting dust?

- What are some of the Bible stories or Scripture verses that really resonate with you? What is it about these verses that reach your soul?

- Do you agree with the author that God did not create sin but created the possibility of sin when God gave humans the freedom to make their own decisions?

- If a nonreligious person asked you what it means for God to be love, how would you respond?

- In what ways do you think Jesus models for us the way God intended for humans to live?

- Do you think it is possible to accomplish all three of Wesley's Gain, Save, and Give principles? Do you find yourself leaning into one of the three areas most often? If so, why do you think that is?

- Do you give the Bible time to speak to you each day? What are your challenges? What are some mechanisms you've put in place in your life to help you listen for God's voice?

- The author presents four important attributes we must develop to allow God to speak to us: humility, open-mindedness, obedience, and determination. Review these, and ask: Which attributes do you possess? Which attributes do you need to better develop? Discuss as a group how you might nurture these attributes in order to grow closer to God.

Closing Prayer (2 minutes)

God, stir within me a passion to read your Scriptures and to regularly meditate on them throughout the days and weeks. I ask that you grant me the ability to understand what I need to put your teachings into practice. Help me to remember that good intentions are worthless unless connected to and rooted in your love and grace. Help the words of the Bible not to be just words on a page, but passageways of mercy into my heart. Amen.

Session 2

RELATIONSHIP WITH SELF: AN INWARD FOCUS

Session 2

RELATIONSHIP WITH SELF: AN INWARD FOCUS

PLANNING THE SESSION

Session Goals

As a result of conversations and activities connected with this session, group members should begin to:

- Understand the relationship between faith and introspection.
- Learn how to be attentive to negative behaviors and patterns.
- Explore how behavior reflects faith and relationship with God.

Section Summary

Section 2 explores the second set of seven of John Wesley's twenty-one questions. These questions address the theme of "Relationship with Self: an Inward Focus." In these questions, Wesley presses us to consider the quality of the interior life: Our thoughts, beliefs, and even whether we get to bed on time. These questions and the accompanying reflections provide opportunities for self-reflection, introspection, and spiritual growth.

Biblical Foundation

Therefore, as God's choice, holy and loved, put on compassion, kindness, humility, gentleness, and patience.

Colossians 3:12

You are the one who created my innermost parts;
> you knit me together while I was still in my mother's womb.

I give thanks to you that I was marvelously set apart.
> Your works are wonderful—I know that very well.

Psalm 139:13-14

I've said these things to you so that you will have peace in me. In the world you have distress. But be encouraged! I have conquered the world.

John 16:33

Do everything without grumbling and arguing so that you may be blameless and pure, innocent children of God surrounded by people who are crooked and corrupt. Among these people you shine like stars in the world because you hold on to the word of life. This will allow me to say on the day of Christ that I haven't run for nothing or worked for nothing.

Philippians 2:14-16

Special Preparation

- Provide writing paper and pens for those who may need them. Also have Bibles available for those who do not bring one.

- Invite participants to read Section 2 in advance of the session.
- Have available large sheets of blank paper or a whiteboard for group activity.
- As leader, you'll want to go over the session in advance and select or adapt the activities you think will work best for your group in the time allotted. Consider your own responses to questions you will pose to the group.
- Make nametags available if desired.

FACILITATING THE SESSION

Welcome and Opening Prayer (3 minutes)

As participants arrive, welcome them to the study and invite them to make use of one of the available Bibles, if they did not bring one. Offer the following prayer, pray one of your own, or invite a group member to pray.

Creator of the universe, we thank you for the gift of life you've entrusted in us. Guard our hearts and attitudes that we may see as you see. Help us find security in you and free us from the need to feel superior. Let us see our place in your kingdom and humble ourselves before our brothers and sisters. Amen.

Video (10 minutes)

Play the video for session 2. The segment discusses how a focus on material things can lead to putting individual wants and needs ahead of God and other relationships. This section reviews Wesley's questions, "Am I a slave to dress, friends, work, or habits?" The author compels us to give an honest examination to our motives and seek forgiveness.

Choose from the following for a brief discussion:

- What things motivate you? In what ways might you be a slave to dress, friends, work, or habits?

- How have you experienced material things getting in the way of your relationship with God and others?
- How can you be real to yourself and real to your growing faith by paying close attention to these questions and the act of introspection?
- What parts of your interior life could use work? What parts feel in line with God and others?

Biblical Foundation (5 minutes)

Read aloud Colossians 3:12 and discuss:

- This verse describes how the Colossians should live as new members of Christ's community. How do we reflect our membership in Christ's community?
- How can we "put on" traits such as "compassion, kindness, humility, gentleness, and patience"?
- Paul calls this community, "God's choice, holy and loved." How does being God's chosen people demand different values and behaviors?

Week in Review (10 minutes)

Section 2 explores the relationship with the self through questions about personal thoughts, beliefs, and behaviors. Review the questions with the group:

1. Am I proud?
2. Am I defeated in any part of my life?
3. Do I go to bed on time and get up on time?
4. Do I grumble or complain constantly?
5. Am I a slave to dress, friends, work, or habits?
6. How do I spend my spare time?
7. Am I self-conscious, self-pitying, or self-justifying?

Invite responses to a few of the prompts below:

- What was your experience moving through the questions this week?
- Which ones stood out to you?
- Which were the most difficult to grapple with?
- Did any of them lead to a sense of transformation as you contemplated them?
- How did living the questions this week have an impact on your relationship with yourself?
- What was your method of engaging the questions?
- Did you read the passages in the morning or the evening?

Group Activity (20 minutes)

The following section provides opportunities for discussion of the week's theme, Relationship with Self, and the seven related questions. Choose from the following activities to find one that best fits your group dynamic.

Questions in Scripture

Use the following Scripture passages for this exercise:

On the sixth day God completed all the work that he had done, and on the seventh day God rested from all the work that he had done. God blessed the seventh day and made it holy, because on it God rested from all the work of creation.

Genesis 2:2-3

Do everything without grumbling and arguing so that you may be blameless and pure, innocent children of God surrounded by people who are crooked and corrupt. Among these people you shine like stars in the world because you hold on to the word of life. This will allow me to say on the day of Christ that I haven't run for nothing or worked for nothing.

Philippians 2:14-16

We didn't bring anything into the world and so we can't take anything out of it: we'll be happy with food and clothing. But people who are trying to get rich fall into temptation. They are trapped by many stupid and harmful passions that plunge people into ruin and destruction.

1 Timothy 6:7-9

Don't do anything for selfish purposes, but with humility think of others as better than yourselves. Instead of each person watching out for their own good, watch out for what is better for others.

Philippians 2:3-4

Create three or four small groups and assign one of the Scripture texts to each. Have posted or hand out the following instructions to each group.

1. Silently skim the assigned passage.
2. Give a short summary of the passage.
3. Answer the following questions:
   o Which of the week's seven questions does the passage most closely relate to?
   o How might the passage guide the development of spiritual practice around this issue?
   o How can the instructions in these Scripture verses become spiritual practices that draw us closer to God?
4. Select three spiritual practices from the Scripture text to share with the larger group.

After the allotted time has passed, call the groups back together to share their findings. On the board or a large sheet of paper, make a list of the various spiritual practices as they are mentioned by each group.

Pale Blue Dot

Print out or display the Voyager 1 photograph of the earth from four billion miles away. You can find it here: http://photojournal .jpl.nasa.gov/jpegMod/PIA00452_modest.jpg. You may also want to invite the class to view the photo on their smartphones.

Share this caption with the group:

> This narrow-angle color image of the Earth, dubbed 'Pale Blue Dot', is a part of the first ever 'portrait' of the solar system taken by Voyager 1. The spacecraft acquired a total of 60 frames for a mosaic of the solar system from a distance of more than 4 billion miles from Earth and about 32 degrees above the ecliptic. From Voyager's great distance Earth is a mere point of light, less than the size of a picture element even in the narrow-angle camera. Earth was a crescent only 0.12 pixel in size. Coincidentally, Earth lies right in the center of one of the scattered light rays resulting from taking the image so close to the sun. This blown-up image of the Earth was taken through three color filters—violet, blue and green—and recombined to produce the color image. The background features in the image are artifacts resulting from the magnification.[1]

Consider that the dot in this photograph has been magnified so that it is visible. How does looking at this photograph make you feel about your day-to-day problems? About your relationship with God? About the things you take pride in?

Honest Answer

Divide the group into pairs. Have one member of each pair ask the other, "How are you doing?" The answer can't just be

"Good" or "Fine"; each participant must share something honest about that day. Instruct each pair to reverse the roles to allow both participants to ask and answer. After each pair takes turns asking and answering, ask everyone to reflect on how it felt to answer the question honestly. What did you learn about the other person that you might not have known? What did you learn about yourself? How might this exercise help you have the courage to reach out in honesty when you feel defeated in your life?

Sleep-Deprived

Divide the whiteboard or a large sheet of paper into two sections: Enough Sleep and Not Enough Sleep. Ask the group to brainstorm about the effects of each of these conditions. Name as many outcomes as possible. Once the board is full, reflect on the pervasive effects. How many aspects of daily life are affected by the quality and quantity of sleep? How would your life be different if you were more intentional about getting enough sleep? What things would change? Would your spiritual life improve?

Spare Time

As a group, brainstorm about the kinds of spare-time activities that bring enjoyment and leave you feeling refreshed and energized. Fill the whiteboard or a large sheet of paper with ideas for what to do with spare time, including both short activities (like taking three to five minutes to pray, as the author does) and longer pursuits (like running, reading a book, or writing in a journal). Compile the list on a sheet of paper and make copies to distribute to the group the following week. For discussion, ask, How much of your spare time do you spend engaged in these pursuits? If it's less than you would like, how can you restructure your time so that you are spending it in ways that bring you life?

Humility in Conversation

Invite the group to divide into pairs with one requirement—everyone must pair up with someone they don't know very well.

Spend a few minutes on introductions and conversation to get comfortable. Have this week's Scripture passage on the whiteboard or large sheet of paper:

> Don't do anything for selfish purposes, but with humility think of others as better than yourselves. Instead of each person watching out for their own good, watch out for what is better for others.
>
> Philippians 2:3-4

Ask each pair to consider the following questions:

- What is a good definition of humility? How is Jesus a model of humility?
- What is the difference between being humble and watching out for others and letting people take advantage of you? How can you strike that balance?
- Think of people in your life you consider to be more important than yourself. What words would you use to describe those relationships? Can you imagine extending that feeling to other people beyond this circle? What about extending it to all other people?
- How does it feel when others put your needs before their own? Can you think of an example?

Ideas for Further Reflection
(additional 30 minutes if needed)

Choose from the following questions to offer the class ways to reflect further on this week's seven questions in the week to come. Alternatively, these questions may be used to supplement the class discussion.

- Consider a news segment together. Which people in the media spotlight today appear to be proud? What behaviors do they display that reinforces this appearance?

- Have each person name one preoccupation that takes up more space than it should in their life. Discuss the factors that might be driving these unhealthy fixations. For example, someone who grew up in poverty might be fixated on financial security to such a degree that it leaves little room for focusing on God's mission. Spend some time helping each other understand the "why" behind the issues.

- Discuss how the people in your group spend their spare time. What are some of the activities you enjoy? Don't enjoy? Do you spend more of your spare time involved in things you like or dislike?

- Tell your group about someone outside the group you find hard to like (keep it anonymous.) Briefly explain why your initial impression is negative. Commit to getting to know this person better over the coming weeks. Ask each other how the relationship is progressing, and what discoveries you are making about yourself and the other person.

- Spend time discussing with each other at least one characteristic about each person in the group that makes them valuable to God and to the group.

- Launch a "no complaining" challenge for your group. Have some fun with it! Decide if your challenge will be for a day, a week, or longer. How will you track it? What will the "winners" receive?

- Do you have anyone in your life who can honestly tell you when you're being prideful? Or do you go on the defense?

- Share a time you've been successful in overcoming a sense of unhealthy pride.

- What's the difference between being prideful and being proud?

- Do you answer honestly when you are asked, "How are you doing?"

- When do you feel defeated in life? What are your mechanisms for overcoming the defeat you are feeling?

- Have you ever encountered a person who was living out his or her job with such positivity and enthusiasm that it turned your day around?

- Identify someone you know who appears to be living within God's will for his or her life. What signs do you see as an onlooker that point to this person being in tune with God's will for him or her?

- What are some activities that you wish you did more of? How can you make changes in your life to make that happen? What can you do for each other in the group to improve the quality of people's spare time?

- Have you ever been the recipient of a random act of kindness? How did that make you feel? Were you suspicious of the person's motives? Did you pass along the favor?

- Raise your hand if you are a control freak. Why do you need to be in control of the remote or the map or the meetings you attend? What is driving that? How can you relinquish control and follow others, even if only occasionally?

Closing Prayer (2 minutes)

God, teach me to serve you first and to seek your kingdom. Help me to be less concerned about myself and more about you and your mission for this world. Help me to be aware of myself, my faults, and my limitations, but also not to be so concerned with myself that I forget your purpose for me. Amen

Session 3

RELATIONSHIP WITH OTHERS: AN OUTWARD FOCUS

Session 3

RELATIONSHIP WITH OTHERS:
AN OUTWARD FOCUS

Session 3

RELATIONSHIP WITH OTHERS: AN OUTWARD FOCUS

PLANNING THE SESSION

Session Goals

As a result of conversations and activities connected with this session, group members should begin to:

- Learn how relationships with others reflect faith in practice.
- Explore the process of incorporating others into your faithful life.
- Discern how to imitate the life of Jesus in relationships with others.

Section Summary

Section 3 explores the final group of seven of John Wesley's twenty-one questions. These questions address the theme of "Relationship with Others: an Outward Focus." Deeply committed Christians are called to take special care of their relationships with other people. Having peaceful relationships at home and in the world is an integral part of God's mission to restore the world to wholeness.

Biblical Foundation

Jesus told this parable to certain people who had convinced themselves that they were righteous and who looked on everyone else with disgust: "Two people went up to the temple to pray. One was a Pharisee and the other a tax collector. The Pharisee stood and prayed about himself with these words, 'God, I thank you that I'm not like everyone else—crooks, evildoers, adulterers—or even like this tax collector. I fast twice a week. I give a tenth of everything I receive.' But the tax collector stood at a distance. He wouldn't even lift his eyes to look toward heaven. Rather, he struck his chest and said, 'God, show mercy to me, a sinner.' I tell you, this person went down to his home justified rather than the Pharisee. All who lift themselves up will be brought low, and those who make themselves low will be lifted up."

Luke 18:9-14

Therefore, go and make disciples of all nations, baptizing them in the name of the Father and of the Son and of the Holy Spirit, teaching them to obey everything that I've commanded you. Look, I myself will be with you every day until the end of this present age.

Matthew 28:19-20

God didn't give us a spirit that is timid but one that is powerful, loving, and self-controlled.

2 Timothy 1:7

My dear friends, since we have these promises, let's cleanse ourselves from anything that contaminates our body or spirit so that we make our holiness complete in the fear of God.

2 Corinthians 7:1

Special Preparation

- Provide writing paper and pens for those who may need them. Also have Bibles available for those who do not bring one.
- Invite participants to read Section 3 in advance of the session and remind them to bring their journals with them.
- Have available large sheets of blank paper (newsprint, poster paper) or a whiteboard for group activity.
- As leader, go over the session in advance and select or adapt the activities you think will work best for your group in the time allotted. Consider your own responses to questions you will pose to the group.
- Make nametags available if desired.

FACILITATING THE SESSION

Welcome and Opening Prayer (3 minutes)

As participants arrive, welcome them to the study and invite them to make use of one of the available Bibles, if they did not bring one. Offer the following prayer, pray one of your own, or invite a group member to pray.

Jesus, you have modeled honesty—from your birth to your death, burial, and resurrection. We pray that honesty may become one of our most valued and tangible virtues. Direct our thoughts, words, and actions that we may enhance all of the relationships we are in—at home, work, school, and places of recreation. Amen.

Video (10 minutes)

Play the video for session 3. The segment reviews the final group of seven questions and recalls that the questions are meant to help us grow in our faith. The author devotes his discussion to the first question, "Do I thank God that I am not like others," which comes directly from the parable of the Pharisee and the tax collector in Luke 18:9-14. Read the parable out loud.

Choose from the following for a brief discussion:

- Answer honestly: Do you ever thank God that you are not like others?
- What does this parable teach about relationships with others?
- How are those relationships related to the relationship with self and God?
- Which character in this parable do you identify with? Why?

Biblical Foundation (5 minutes)

The author, Chris Folmsbee, identifies two key acts for performing the gospel. The first is to serve through acts of mercy and compassion. The second is to attack and destroy systems of injustice in the world.

Read aloud the biblical passage Matthew 28:19-20, which is known as the Great Commission.

- How does this passage connect with the author's words about serving through mercy and compassion and attacking systems of injustice?
- How might speaking about one's faith live into the call of the Great Commission?
- How are we assured in this passage that we can fulfill the Great Commission?

Week in Review (10 minutes)

Section 3 explores the nature of the relationship with others by asking questions about mind-set, behavior, and faith experience. Review the questions with the group:

1. Do I thank God that I am not like others?
2. Am I consciously or unconsciously creating the impression that I am better than I am? In other words, am I a hypocrite?
3. Do I confidentially pass on to others what was told to me in confidence?
4. Am I jealous, impure, critical, irritable, touchy, or distrustful?
5. Am I honest in all my actions and words or do I exaggerate?
6. Is there anyone whom I fear, dislike, disown, criticize, hold resentment toward, or disregard?
7. When did I last speak to someone about my faith?

Invite responses to a few of the prompts below:

- What was your experience moving through the questions this week?
- Which ones stood out to you?
- Which were the most difficult to grapple with?
- Did any of them lead to a sense of transformation as you contemplated them?
- How did living the questions this week have an impact on your relationships with others?
- What was your method of engaging the questions?
- Did you read the passages in the morning or the evening?

Group Activity (20 minutes)

Explore the content of section 3 together with the following exercises:

Two Truths and a Lie

Go around the room and have each person tell three things about themselves. Two of the statements should be true, and one is something they wish could be true. Keep the exaggerated version close enough to the truth to be believable. Have the rest of the participants guess which one is the exaggeration.

How did it feel telling an exaggerated version of the truth and having class members wonder if it were true? The next time you are tempted to lie or exaggerate, stop to notice what is driving this temptation. Are you intimidated by the group or person you are with? Do you feel "less than" them in some way? Are you trying to impress someone?

Unafraid

Have the following Scripture passages posted on the whiteboard or a large sheet of paper so the class can see:

> God didn't give us a spirit that is timid but one that is
> powerful, loving, and self-controlled.
>
> 2 Timothy 1:7

> If Timothy comes to you, be sure that he has no reason
> to be afraid while he's with you, because he does he work
> of the Lord just like I do.
>
> 1 Corinthians 16:10

Explain that these two verses are related because both include Paul's counsel to Timothy on the importance of being unafraid. Remind the group of the second question in the third section, "Am I consciously or unconsciously creating the impression that

I am better than I am? In other words, am I a hypocrite?" What is the relationship between fearlessness and being one's authentic self? Why was it so important to Paul that Timothy have a powerful spirit and resist being afraid? Can you think of examples in your own life where you've "faked it" and presented yourself falsely? How might this be evidence of a timid spirit?

Naming Our Faults

Question 18: Am I jealous, impure, critical, irritable, touchy, or distrustful?

Consider the following Scripture passage:

Patience leads to abundant understanding,
　　but impatience leads to stupid mistakes.
A peaceful mind gives life to the body,
　　but jealousy rots the bones.

Proverbs 14:29-30

The behaviors John Wesley named in this question live inside all of us. We don't like that we possess these types of behavior, but we do. We work on becoming less of all of the above, because when we express them, they have an adverse impact on our lives and the lives of others around us. That's why God calls us to grow in our capacity to live above and beyond the above characteristics, and ones like them.

Do you know people who "fly off the handle?" What drives their behavior? Do you have a close relationship with anyone who displays any of these behaviors regularly? What is the impact of that person on you when he or she behaves in these ways? How do you manage your interactions with him or her?

Which of the characteristics that John Wesley calls out in this question do you struggle with the most?

Love and Separation

Have someone read the following Scripture verses aloud to the group:

> Love should be shown without pretending. Hate evil, and hold on to what is good. Love each other like the members of your family. Be the best at showing honor to each other. Don't hesitate to be enthusiastic—be on fire in the Spirit as you serve the Lord! Be happy in your hope, stand your ground when you're in trouble, and devote yourselves to prayer. Contribute to the needs of God's people, and welcome strangers into your home. Bless people who harass you—bless and don't curse them. Be happy with those who are happy, and cry with those who are crying. Consider everyone as equal, and don't think that you're better than anyone else. Instead, associate with people who have no status. Don't think that you're so smart. Don't pay back anyone for their evil actions with evil actions, but show respect for what everyone else believes is good.
>
> Romans 12:9-17

How can living out these spiritual principles produce a positive response to the question, "Is there anyone whom I fear, dislike, disown, criticize, hold resentment toward, or disregard?" Have you created or kept separation between yourself and another person because you simply don't like them? If so, ask yourself what is driving this dislike. More broadly, would you say you are at peace with God, self, and others? Why or why not?

Speaking of Faith

When did you last speak to someone about your faith? When John Wesley faces listeners with this question, he is directly encouraging them to take up the challenge Jesus gave his disciples in Acts 1:8, to be his witnesses or storytellers. To respond faithfully to Wesley's question is to live a life of going, obeying, and listening to the Holy Spirit, realizing that each one of us is sent into the world to be the hands and feet of Jesus.

When did you last speak to someone about your faith? Do you show your faith more through your words or deeds? How can you balance both of those sides of the gospel "coin" in your day-to-day life? Think through your story of personal transformation. How has your faith in God changed your life and made you a better person with a better effect on the life of others?

Ideas for Further Reflection (additional 30 minutes if needed)

Choose from the following questions to offer the class ways to reflect further on this week's seven questions in the week to come. Alternatively, these questions may be used to supplement the class discussion.

- Pretend you are outsiders, looking in at your lives. What judgments could you be making about yourselves?

- Discuss a public figure who is known as a famous or infamous "liar." (There are plenty of subjects out there to choose from.) Talk about what drove that person to lie and imagine alternatives if the truth had been lived instead.

- Have each person in the group share a story of becoming overcome with compassion. Discuss how this helps all of us overcome selfishness or conceit.

- Tell your group your faith story. What has been your "before and after" experience of transformation? Make a goal to tell this to one person outside your group this week. What will that be like? How will you choose the right moment?

- Select a person who is receiving notoriety in the media right now. Discuss the things that are being said about this person. Have you compared yourself to them in any way? (For instance, have you said to yourself, "I would never do what he or she did" or "I would never say something like that")? Are you deriving any satisfaction from the negative things that are being said about this person? Are you contributing to the negativity in any way (such as posting comments or sharing news clips)? How are you justifying this satisfaction?

- Has anyone ever betrayed your confidence? Share your stories and discuss what happened after you discovered that your trust was broken.

- Why are humans so prone to gossip? Why do we seek to hold power through information? How do the environments in which we work, live, and play affect this dynamic?

- Recall a time when you felt distrustful of a person or a group of people. In retrospect, was that distrust justified? Did it lead to other negative emotions in your life? Would you handle any of the events differently if they occurred today?

- Recall a time from your childhood when you were caught in a lie. Why did you lie? How did the person who confronted you behave? Were you punished or extended grace?

- Has anyone ever confessed a lie to you? Were you able to forgive this person for the transgression, or are you still carrying the hurt? Why did this person deceive you?

- Are there people in your life that you find it difficult to spend time with because of their personality or disposition? What do you think Jesus would say to you about this?

- Are you guilty of comparing yourself to others and, therefore, thinking you might be better than another person? What is the difference between compassion and comparison?

- How did you come to faith? Who shared their faith with you, and was it through words, deeds, or both?

- How are you sharing your faith with others? Would your coworkers and neighbors say you were a Christian? How would they know?

- What are good, productive ways to share your faith, and what are some methods that might drive people away?

Closing Prayer (2 minutes)

Lord, change us. Remove the tendency for us to compare ourselves with others and think we are better than they are. Replace comparison with compassion and make us more like Christ is—loving to all. Jesus, we pray that we may be reconciled to all those toward whom we hold resentment or dislike. Amen.

HOW TO START
AN ACCOUNTABILITY GROUP

HOW TO START
AN ACCOUNTABILITY GROUP

In 1729, John and Charles Wesley formed an accountability group in Christ Church, Oxford, England. The "Holy Club," as it was mockingly called by other students and faculty, was dedicated to Bible study, serving the poor, giving to those in need, visiting prisoners, reading the classics and talking about them together, fasting, and prayer. John Wesley led the Holy Club until 1735.

The Holy Club never exceeded twenty-five members. A key component to the group's spiritual practice was the daily consideration of questions like the ones that have formed the basis for this study. These soul-searching inquiries were meant to bring the members of the club into more meaningful relationship with God, self, and others. Group members would use the questions in their private devotions and then discuss them together when they met. This way of "methodically" examining their spiritual lives earned them the name *methodists*.

The original Holy Club met three or four evenings a week, studied the classics, and read a book about divinity on Sundays. Later, they set aside time for prayer, spiritual development, Bible study, and talking together. They celebrated Holy Communion and fasted on Wednesdays and Fridays until 3 p.m. They distributed meals to the poor, visited prisoners, and taught orphans how to read. The Holy Club was a combination of service to the community and spiritual accountability to one another.

John Wesley drew up these initial rules in 1738 to establish "Six Preconditions for Participation in a Community Seeking a Holy Life":

> The design of our meeting is, to obey that command of God, "Confess your faults one to another, and pray for one another, that ye may be healed." To this end, we intend—
>
> 1. To meet once a week, at the least.
> 2. To come punctually at the hour appointed, without some extraordinary reason.
> 3. To begin (those of us who are present) exactly at the hour, with singing or prayer.
> 4. To speak each of us in order, freely and plainly, the true state of our souls, with the faults we have committed in thought, word, or deed, and the temptations we have felt, since our last meeting.
> 5. To end every meeting with prayer, suited to the state of each person present.
> 6. To desire some person among us; to speak his own state first, and then to ask the rest, in order, as many and as searching questions as may be, concerning their state, sins, and temptations.[1]

If you would like to start a kind of Holy Club in your church or community, consider the following guidelines in addition to Wesley's original instructions:

- Keep the number small. If you allow five minutes for each person to share, a one-hour meeting could work for twelve people. However, a group of this size may make it hard for the members to form friendships and grow to trust one another.
- Include members who are genuinely devoted to working through the twenty-one questions and performing acts of community service.
- It is not necessary for members to know one another before joining the group.
- Decide whether the club will meet once or twice a week, or even more.

- Secure a time and place for meetings well in advance. The space should be private so members feel comfortable sharing personal information.
- Multiply the number of members by five to figure out the ideal length of a meeting. For example, a meeting with six members should last thirty minutes.
- Ask all members to commit to being on time and keeping the confidences of the other members.

Once you have settled the logistical details, prepare for the first meeting. The following structure might be useful, but feel free to alter it to fit the character of your group.

- Open the meeting with prayer. The prayers of John Wesley make fine choices, or you can ask a member of the group to offer a prayer.

I am no longer my own, but yours.
Put me to what you will,
rank me with whom you will;
put me to doing,
put me to suffering;
let me be employed for you,
or laid aside for you,
exalted for you,
or brought low for you;
let me be full,
let me be empty,
let me have all things,
let me have nothing:
I freely and wholeheartedly yield all things
to your pleasure and disposal.
And now, glorious and blessed God,
Father, Son and Holy Spirit,
you are mine and I am yours. So be it.
And the covenant now made on earth, let it be ratified in heaven.
Amen.[2]

Holy God whose nature and name is Love:
Seeing there is in Christ Jesus an infinite fullness
of all that we can want or wish
O that we may all receive of his fullness,
grace upon grace;
Grace to pardon our sins and subdue our iniquities;
Grace to justify our persons and to sanctify our souls;
Grace to complete that holy change,
that renewal of our hearts,
whereby we may be transformed
into that blessed image wherein you did create us;
through Jesus Christ our Lord,
who lives and reigns with you and the Holy Spirit,
one God, now and forever.
Amen.[3]

- It is most efficient for a group to focus on one of the twenty-one questions per meeting. Have a member read that question out loud to the group.

- Invite group members to share about their experience working with that question during the time since the last meeting. Group members may share weaknesses and specifically ask for ways the group can hold them accountable to the question.

- The leader or others may ask questions to prompt discussion:
  o What is God teaching you through this question?
  o How do you see God working in your situation?
  o How is God encouraging you through this experience?
  o How can the group help you in this moment?

- Read out loud the question the group will consider for the next meeting.

- Set aside five to ten minutes at the end of the meeting to discuss plans for community service or to reflect on that week's service effort.

- Close the meeting with prayer or Scripture. James 5:
  15-16, 19-20 and Hebrews 10:22-25 provide encouraging
  words for those working for accountability.

Prayer that comes from faith will heal the sick, for the
Lord will restore them to health. And if they have sinned,
they will be forgiven. For this reason, confess your sins
to each other and pray for each other so that you may be
healed. The prayer of the righteous person is powerful in
what it can achieve....

My brothers and sisters, if any of you wander from the
truth and someone turns back the wanderer, recognize
that whoever brings a sinner back from the wrong path
will save them from death and will bring about the
forgiveness of many sins.

James 5:15-16, 19-20

Therefore, let's draw near with a genuine heart with the
certainty that our faith gives us, since our hearts are
sprinkled clean from an evil conscience and our bodies
are washed with pure water.

Let's hold on to the confession of our hope without
wavering, because the one who made the promises is
reliable.

And let us consider each other carefully for the purpose
of sparking love and good deeds. Don't stop meeting
together with other believers, which some people have
gotten into the habit of doing. Instead, encourage each
other, especially as you see the day drawing near.

Hebrews 10:22-25

NOTES

Session 2

1. http://visibleearth.nasa.gov/view.php?id=52392.

How to Start an Accountability Group

1. Thomas C. Oden, ed., *John Wesley's Teachings*, vol 4., *Ethics and Society* (Grand Rapids: Zondervan, 2014), 29-31.

2. http://www.methodist.org.uk/who-we-are/what-is-distinctive -about-methodism/a-covenant-with-god.

3. https://www.umcdiscipleship.org/resources/celebration-of-john -wesley-in-word-and-song-on-the-300th-anniversary-of-his.

CPSIA information can be obtained
at www.ICGtesting.com
Printed in the USA
LVHW100918210322
R17224400001B/R172244PG713749LVX00001B/1

9 781501 832925